WORKBOOKS

K

Printing

Handwriting

Author Brenda Apsley
Consultant Linda Ruggieri

DK

Editors Jolyon Goddard,
Nandini Gupta, Margaret Parrish
Art Editors Kanika Kalra, Roohi Rais
Art Director Martin Wilson
Senior Producer, Pre-Production Francesca Wardell
Producer Priscilla Reby
DTP Designer Anita Yadav
Managing Editor Soma B. Chowdhury
Managing Art Editor Ahlawat Gunjan

First American Edition, 2016
Published in the United States by DK Publishing
345 Hudson Street, New York, New York 10014

A catalog record for this book
is available from the Library of Congress.
ISBN: 978-1-4654-4469-1

DK books are available at special discounts when purchased
in bulk for sales promotions, premiums, fund-raising, or
educational use. For details, contact: DK Publishing Special
Markets, 345 Hudson Street, New York, New York 10014
SpecialSales@dk.com

Printed and bound in China

All images © Dorling Kindersley Limited
For further information see: www.dkimages.com

A WORLD OF IDEAS:
SEE ALL THERE IS TO KNOW

www.dk.com

Contents

This chart lists all the topics in the book.
Once you have completed each page,
stick a star in the correct box below.

Handwriting Patterns

Write over the yellow lines and then connect the dots.
Begin at the top of the page from the dog to the bone
and from the mouse to the cheese. Follow the direction
shown by the arrows.

Write over the yellow lines and then connect the dots to finish the patterns. Copy the shapes between the lines below.
Remember: Do not lift your pencil from the paper until the end of each line.

Write the shapes on the sheet.

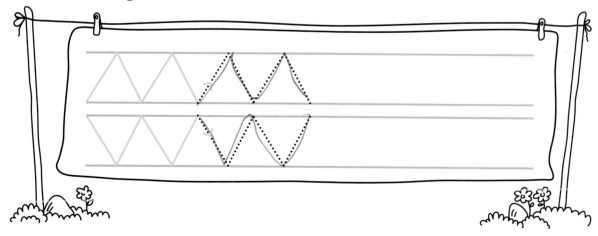

FACTS

Groups of letters that have similar shapes, curves, or lines are sometimes called letter families.

Write the letters with round shapes. Trace each letter.
Then write more letters on each line until you fill the line.
Start at the dots and follow the arrows.

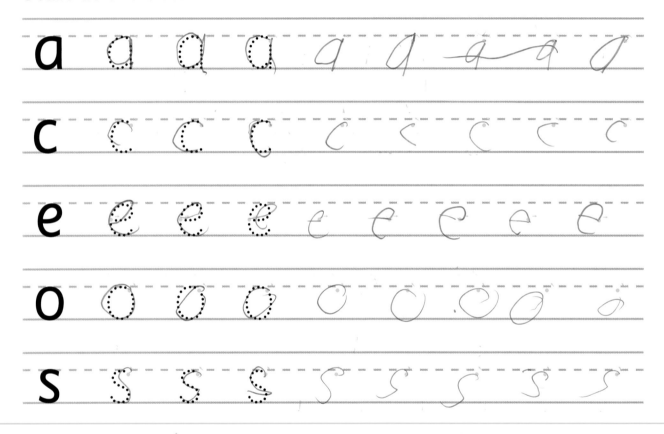

Write round letters to finish the picture.

The letters **d**, **g**, and **q** begin with a round shape. Trace the letter **d** by starting at the dots and following the arrows. Write more letters until you fill the line.

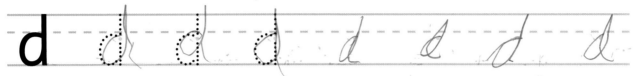

Write the letters **g** and **q**. Trace them by starting at the dots and following the arrows. Write more letters on each line.
Remember: The round part of each letter sits on the line. The bottom part goes down under the line.

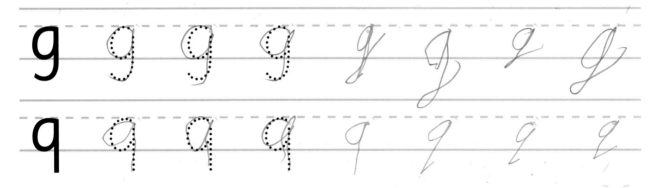

The letter **g** looks like a hook. Trace the letter **g**. Then write the letter **g** three more times to finish the picture. Start each letter from the end of the fishing line.

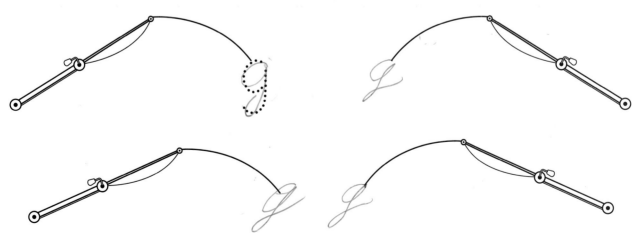

Write the letters **f**, **l**, and **t**. Trace them and then write more letters to fill the lines. Start at the dots and follow the arrows for direction. **Remember:** Write the bar or the line that goes across the letters **f** and **t**, last.

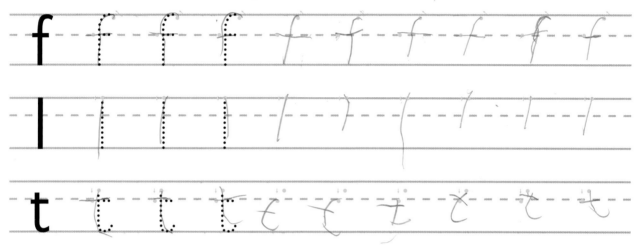

Write the letters **i** and **j**. Trace them and then write more letters to fill the lines. Start at the dots and follow the arrows for direction. **Remember:** Write the dots on the letters **i** and **j** last.

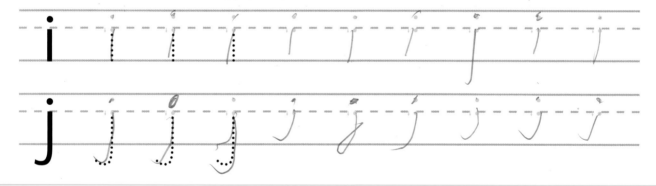

Trace the letters **j** and **t**.
Then write the letters again
to make pairs.

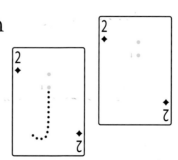
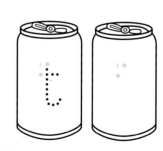

Write the letters **m**, **n**, and **r**. Trace them and then write more letters to fill the lines. Start at the dots and follow the arrows for direction. **Remember:** Your letters should all be the same height.

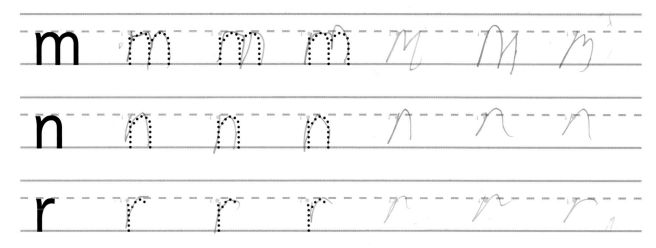

Write the letters **m**, **n**, and **r** to continue the patterns on the flags.

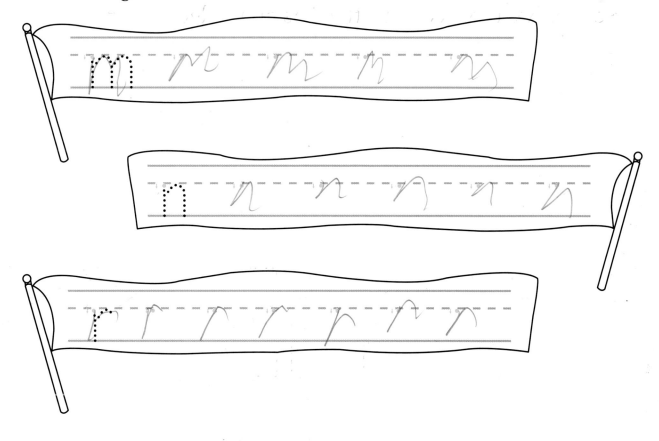

Write the letters **b** and **h**. Trace them and then write more letters to fill the lines. Start at the dots and follow the arrows for direction. **Remember:** Your letters should all be the same height.

Write the letter **k**. Trace it and then write more letters to fill the line. Start at the dots and follow the arrows for direction.

Write the letter **p**. Trace it and then write more letters to fill the line. Start at the dots and follow the arrows for direction.

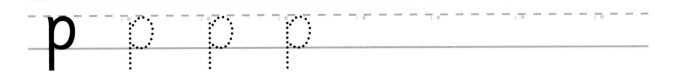

Write the letter **b** on the shopping bags.

  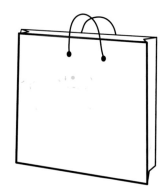

Write the straight-line letters **v**, **w**, **x**, and **z**. Trace them and then write more letters to fill the lines. Start at the dots and follow the arrows for direction.

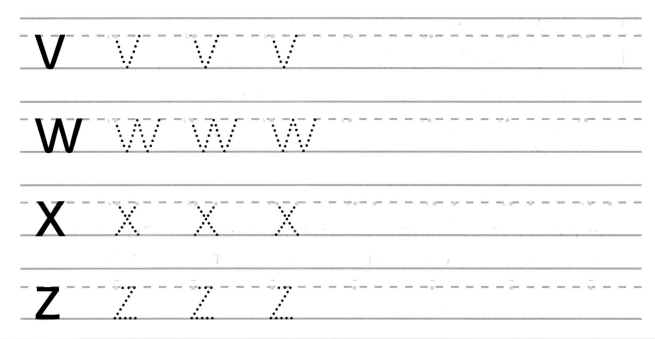

Write the letters **u** and **y**. Trace them and then write more letters to fill the lines. Start at the dots and follow the arrows for direction.

Copy the letters again.

u v w x y z

Trace each letter of the alphabet and then write it two more times. **Remember:** The alphabet is all the letters we use to make words.

Trace the letters of the alphabet in order. Write as neatly as you can. **Remember:** Some lowercase letters go up to the top line (l); some go halfway up (a); some have parts that are round (c, o); and some have parts that are straight and parts that are round (b and d).

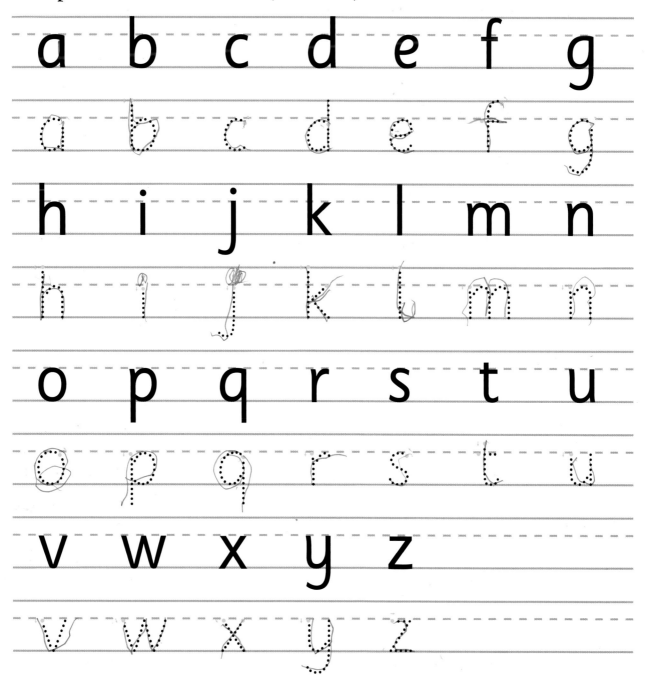

Use the correct letter from the box to begin each word below.
Then write the whole word.

b	r	h	p

bug _ug

bug

pen _en

pen

rug _ug

rug

hen _en

hen

Write a word to label each picture. Choose words from the box.

mug	bed	bun	cat	web	cap

cat

bun

cap

web

bed

Write these words that have the letter **a** in the middle.
They all make the short "a" sound, as heard in "bat."
Write each word three times.

cap

mat   *cat*   *mat*   *man*

man   *cat*   *mat*   *man*
        cat   *mat*   *man*

Copy the label for each picture in your best handwriting.

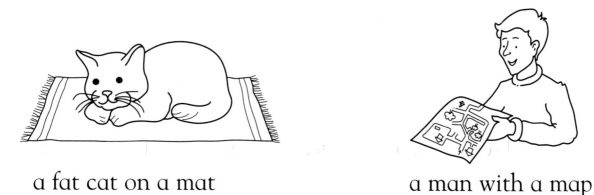

a fat cat on a mat   a man with a map

Complete this list of words by writing the letter **a** in the middle.

Words with **a**			
f __ n	h __ t	b __ t	sn __ p
s __ t	t __ g	t __ p	h __ m
j __ m	p __ t	n __ p	b __ g

Complete each row by writing a word with the letter **e** in the middle. Then copy all the words in your best handwriting on the lines below. **Remember:** The words in each row should rhyme. The endings of these words should sound the same.

yet   set   ...... e ......

....

led   fed   ...... e ......

....

Copy the label for each picture in your best handwriting.

a pet hen

....

Ted in bed

Copy the label. Then draw its picture above.

ten pens

....

Write these words that have the letter **i** in the middle.
They all make the short "i" sound, as heard in "pin."

fin

....

sit

....

bib

....

Complete this list of words by writing the letter **i** in the middle.

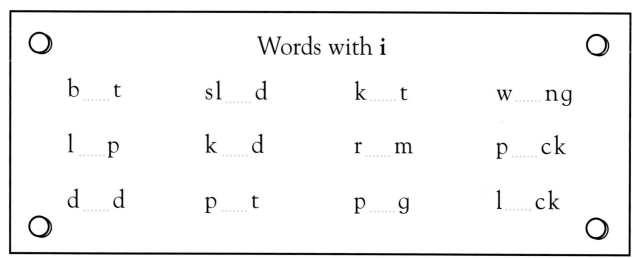

Words with **i**

b ... t	sl ... d	k ... t	w ... ng
l ... p	k ... d	r ... m	p ... ck
d ... d	p ... t	p ... g	l ... ck

Write two words to label each picture. You can use the words given in the box below.

bin	big	wig	lid

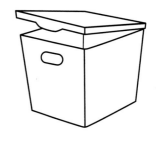

....

Complete the row by writing a word with the letter **o** in the middle. Then write all the words in your best handwriting on the lines. **Remember:** The words in the row should rhyme. Their endings should sound the same.

dot   pot   .... o ....

....

Write a label for each picture. Try to write more than one word for each label. Use words from the box and other words of your own.

| toy   log   rock   boy   dots   dog   frog   box |

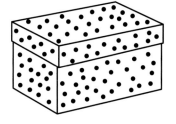

....

....

Write these words that have the letter **u** in the middle. They all make the short "u" sound, as heard in "bun."

fun ....

tub ....

bud ....

jug ....

Write a label for each picture. Try to write more than one word for each label. Use the **u** words from the box and other words of your own.

| pup | bug | rug | cup |

....

Copy the word and draw a picture of it.

sun ....

Some words have two or more letters whose sounds blend together. You can hear the sound of each letter. Letter blends include **bl** in the word "blue" and **fl** in the word "flower."

Copy these letter blends that start words.

bl   fr   gr   cr   sl   sc   st   sm   sn   sp

....

Copy these letter blends that end words.

ft   nt   xt   lf   ct   lt   pt   nd   lp   st

....

Copy these words that have letter blends.

spot   ....   flag   ....   band   ....

frog   ....   fact   ....   next   ....

star   ....   brick   ....   snake   ....

Write these words that have letter blends. Then circle the letter blends at the beginning or end of each word.

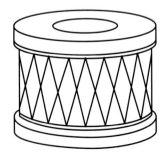

drum

....

nest

....

Some words end in two consonants. Those final consonants may be the same letter twice, as in "bell," or be different, as in "jump."

Copy these words that end with two letters that are the same.

off ....   puff ....   bell ....

pull ....   dress ....   kiss ....

Copy these words that end with **ck**, **mp**, and **ng**.

sock ....   wing ....   duck ....

jump ....   sing ....   ring ....

Write labels for the pictures. Use the words from above.

....

....

Write each word three times on the lines below.
Remember: Always write the word "I" as an uppercase (big) letter. For example, "I like to write words."

I   ....

me   ....

he   ....

we   ....

she   ....

Write labels for this family. Choose words from the box.

mom	dad	baby	girl

Write your first name.   ....

Write your last name.   ....

A compound word is formed by joining two words together to make one new word. For example, "grand" + "mother" = "grandmother."

Write each set of words as one word on the lines below.

tea　　+　pot　　　=　...

post　　+　man　　=　...

butter　+　fly　　　=　...

sun　　+　flower　=　...

lady　　+　bug　　=　...
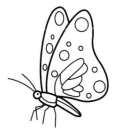

sea　　+　horse　=　...

cup　　+　cake　　=　...

tooth　+　brush　=　...

gold　　+　fish　　=　...

Write each classroom word three times. Try to keep your handwriting the same size as the words you are copying.

book ....

desk ....

chair ....

pencil ....

clock ....

paints ....

bin ....

teacher ....

paper ....

bag ....

Write labels for the pictures.

....

Write the color words below three times.

red

green

yellow

blue

black

white

orange

pink

brown

gray

The word "blue" begins with a blend. Write four other color words that begin with a blend.

Complete the following sentence.

My favorite color is .... because ....

....

Numerals are the symbols we use for numbers.

Write the numerals from 0 to 20 on the lines below.
Note: Sometimes 4 is also written as 4.

0	1	2	3	4	5	6	7	8	9	10

11	12	13	14	15	16	17	18	19	20

Write the number words from zero to twenty.

zero	....		
one	....	eleven	....
two	....	twelve	....
three	....	thirteen	....
four	....	fourteen	....
five	....	fifteen	....
six	....	sixteen	....
seven	....	seventeen	....
eight	....	eighteen	....
nine	....	nineteen	....
ten	....	twenty	....

Write a number word label for each numeral shown on the balloons. One has been done for you.

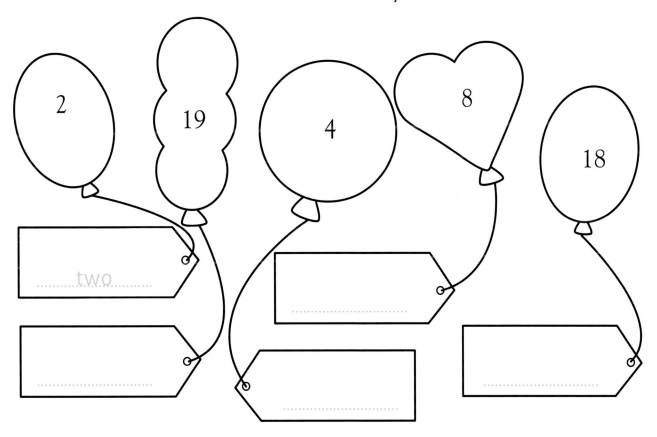

two

Write how old you are. Write the numeral on the card and the number word on the line below. Then count the candles on the cake and write the number word on the line below.

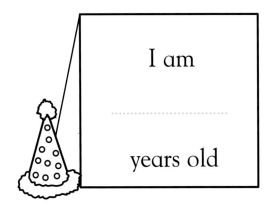

I am

years old

FACTS

Different spelling patterns can make the same sound.
For example, the "ai" sound, as heard in "main," can also
be spelled "ay," as in "say," and "a_e," as in "late."

Copy these words that have the "ai" sound,
as heard in "train."

tail .... rain ....

day .... plate ....

Copy these words that have the "ee" sound, as heard in "meet."

seat .... neat .... feel ....

sheep .... seed .... bean ....

Copy these words that have the "ie" sound, as heard in "lie."

tie .... nine .... bite ....

Write the correct word under each picture.
Use words from the box.

| tree | five | snail |

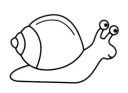      

....

Copy these words that have the "oa" sound, as heard in "coat."

home	moat	goat ....
low	road	note ....
soap	snow	show ....

Copy these words that have the "oo" sound, as heard in "soon."

moon	spoon	bloom ....
blue	true	glue ....
flew	rule	pool ....

Copy these sentences in your best handwriting.
Remember: A sentence begins with an uppercase letter and ends with a period.

The dish ran away with the spoon.

....

....

The goat plays in the snow.

....

....

Sometimes the letters **ar** make the sound heard in the word "car." Write the words with the "ar" sound below three times.

farm   ....

art   ....

cart   ....

chart ....

barn   ....

bark   ....

shark ....

party ....

sharp ....

Write the word with the "ar" sound that names each picture.

....

 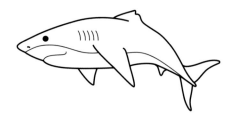

....

Copy these words with the short "oo" sound, as heard in "good."

hood .... wood .... could ....

push .... pull .... would ....

wool .... full .... should ....

Copy these words with the "oy" sound, as heard in "toy."

boy .... boil .... soil ....

joy .... foil .... coil ....

coin .... spoil .... enjoy ....

Copy these words with the "ow" sound, as heard in "now."

out .... town .... towel ....

cow .... loud .... found ....

owl .... now .... shout ....

Write the words for the two pictures.

....

FACTS

Uppercase letters are big letters. Some words, such as "I," the names of people (John), and the names of places (Arizona), begin with uppercase letters. Uppercase letters are also called capital letters.

Write the alphabet in uppercase letters on the lines.
Start at the dots and follow the arrows for direction.
Remember: The alphabet starts with **A** and ends with **Z**.

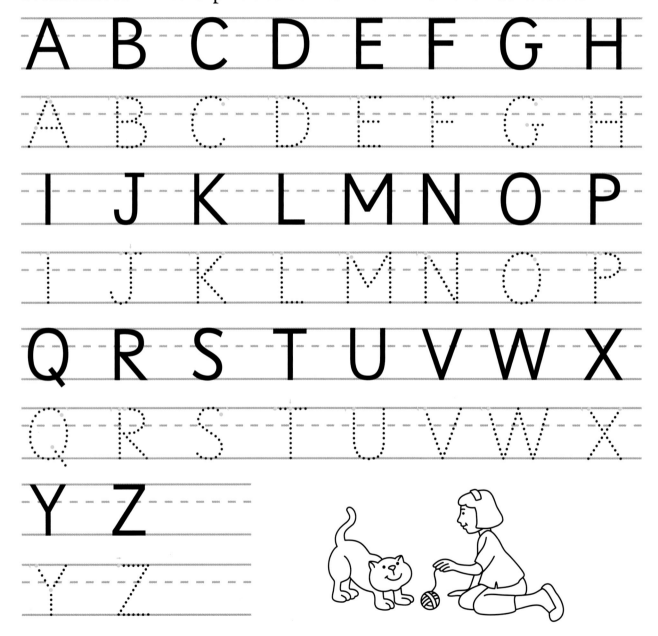

A B C D E F G H

A B C D E F G H

I J K L M N O P

I J K L M N O P

Q R S T U V W X

Q R S T U V W X

Y Z

Y Z

Proper nouns are words that name people and places. They always begin with an uppercase letter.

Write these names in your best handwriting.

Eric .... Will ....

Tom .... Mel ....

Sam .... Lucy ....

Katy .... Ben ....

Tim .... Jemma ....

Write your name. ....

Make a list of your friends' names.

My Friends

A lowercase letter is written on each flower. Write the uppercase form of the letter on the leaves of each flower, as shown for the letter **a**.

A sentence is a group of words that forms a complete thought. Every sentence starts with an uppercase letter and ends with a period (**.**), a question mark (**?**), or an exclamation point (**!**).

Write these sentences in your best handwriting.

I like plums. ....

I can jump. ....

I like to write. ....

Write these words as sentences. **Remember:** You may want to put a finger-width space between each word to make your writing easier to read.

i just won the trophy

....

how old is dan

....

i like my new bike

....

the cat is black

....

The names of the days of the week are proper nouns. Each starts with an uppercase letter.

Copy the names of the days of the week in your neatest handwriting. Write each name twice.

Sunday   ....

Monday   ....

Tuesday   ....

Wednesday   ....

Thursday   ....

Friday   ....

Saturday   ....

Write the name of the day that comes after Friday. ....

Which days begin with **T**? ....

On which days do you go to school? ....

....

What is the day today? Write what you have done so far today.

....

....

....

Copy the names of the months of the year twice.
Remember: Months are proper nouns. They start with an uppercase letter.

January

February

March

April

May

June

July

August

September

October

November

December

The title of a book, story, or rhyme is its name. Write these titles in your best handwriting. **Remember:** Begin main words in titles with uppercase letters.

James and the Giant Peach

....

Old Macdonald Had a Farm

....

Write a title for each cover from the list below.

Old King Cole   In a Dark, Dark Wood

Goldilocks and
the Three Bears

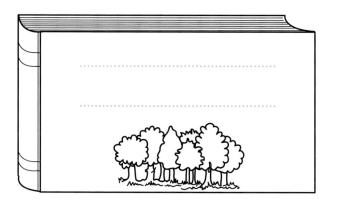

Draw a picture and copy the poem in your best handwriting. Begin by writing the title. **Remember:** Write in uppercase and lowercase letters. Use commas and periods.

Little Wind

Little wind, blow on the hilltop,
Little wind, blow on the plain,
Little wind, blow up the sunshine,
Little wind, blow off the rain.

Anonymous

A comma is a punctuation mark that is used to show a break in the sentence or a slight pause. Commas are also used to separate words in a list. For example, "I like apples, bananas, and cherries."

The commas in this rhyme show you when to pause. Copy the rhyme in your best handwriting.

Puppy Dogs

One little, two little,
Three little puppy dogs,
Four little, five little,
Six little puppy dogs.

....

....

....

....

Copy these sentences and add the missing commas.

I like the colors red green yellow and blue.

....

I know children named Abby Ben and Dan.

....

FACTS

A question mark (**?**) is used in a sentence that asks a question. An exclamation point (**!**) shows anger, pain, danger, or excitement.

Rewrite each sentence with a question mark or an exclamation point at the end.

Do you like apples

....

That ride was exciting

....

Give me my ball back

....

Write these words that ask questions.

who ....   why ....   what ....

how ....   when ....   where ....

Use words from above to complete the questions below.
Remember: Begin each sentence with an uppercase letter.

.... is your name?

.... old are you?

.... is my pail?

Books that are made up are called fiction. The stories are not real. Books that are true are called nonfiction. They give information and facts.

Copy these book titles using uppercase and lowercase letters.
Remember: The title is the name of the book.

Fiction	**Nonfiction**
The Ugly Duckling	My Book of Space
....	....
The Snowman	How to Draw
....	....
Old Bear	Learn about Tigers
....	....
The Worst Witch	Fun with Numbers
....	....

Find the title on the list above and write it on each book cover.

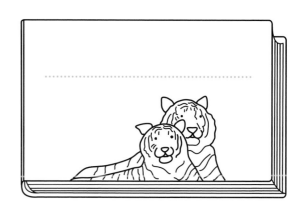

Write a short story in your best handwriting. Look at the pictures and write a sentence about each one. Use the words given in the box. **Remember:** A sentence begins with an uppercase letter and ends with a period, question mark, or exclamation point.

boy	girl	build	snowman	night	day

Title: ....

....

....

....

....

A dictionary is a book that tells you what words mean.

baby	A baby is a very young child.
bag	A bag is used to carry things.
ball	A ball is something round that rolls.
bank	A bank is a place where people keep money.
bark	A bark is the noise a dog makes. Bark is the outside part of a tree.
bat	A bat is used to hit a ball. A bat is a small animal that flies at night.

Write the meanings of these words using the dictionary page above. **Remember:** Some words have more than one meaning. Use each picture to help you find the correct meaning.

Word	Meaning
bat	....
	....
bag	....
	....
bark	....
	....

Write each word in the correct topic box.
Use your neatest handwriting.

shark   robin   beak   fins   flock

crab   whale   nest

feathers   squid   fish   wings

Birds

....

....

....

....

....

....

Sea Animals

....

....

....

....

....

....

Write about yourself in your best handwriting and draw a picture. **Remember:** Proper nouns begin with uppercase letters.

Name: ....

Street: ....

Town or city: ....

State: ....

Zip code: ....

Age: ....

Date of birth: ....

School: ....

Grade: ....

Favorite subject: ....

Teacher's name: ....

Certificate

Congratulations to

....

for successfully
finishing this book.

GOOD JOB!

You're a star.

Date

....

Answer Section with Parents' Notes

This book is intended to introduce printed handwriting skills to your child. The content features English language arts activities appropriate for kindergarten and in line with Common Core State Standards. Working through the activities will help your child to develop a neat style of printing with regular letter formation and size.

Contents

The activities are intended to be completed by a child with adult support. In this book your child will practice:

- handwriting patterns;
- letter shapes;
- writing the lowercase alphabet;
- writing the uppercase alphabet;
- writing letters with ascenders and descenders;
- writing numerals and number words;
- writing words with different vowel sounds;
- writing words with letter blends and double consonants;
- writing compound words;
- writing sentences;
- using basic punctuation, and more.

How to Help Your Child

As you work through the pages with your child, make sure he or she understands what each activity requires. Read the facts, if present, and instructions aloud. Encourage questions and reinforce observations that will build confidence and increase active participation in classes at school.

Encourage your child to write slowly and neatly. Follow the handwriting style taught at your child's school. Point out any mistakes or incorrect letter formations and correct any spelling errors.

In addition to making corrections, it is very important to praise your child's efforts and achievements. Good luck, and remember to have fun!

4

★ Handwriting Patterns

Write over the yellow lines and then connect the dots.
Begin at the top of the page from the dog to the bone
and from the mouse to the cheese. Follow the direction
shown by the arrows.

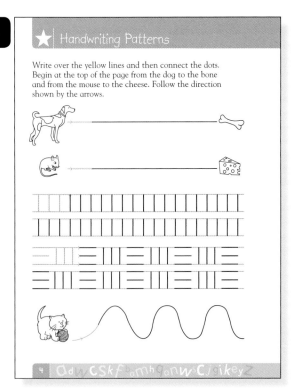

The activities in this book are progressive, so
your child should work from the front to the
back. Provide a comfortable place to sit and
a flat work surface. Encourage your child to
develop a relaxed pencil grip.

5

Letter Shapes ★

Write over the yellow lines and then connect the dots to
finish the patterns. Copy the shapes between the lines below.
Remember: Do not lift your pencil from the paper until
the end of each line.

Write the shapes on the sheet.

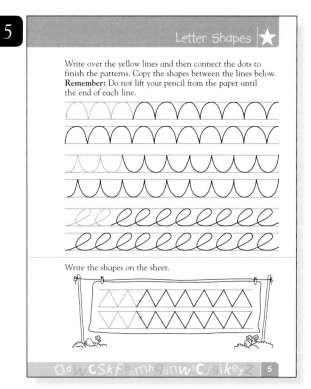

Follow the style of handwriting taught in your
school district. Encourage your child to write
smooth and fluid lines without lifting the pencil
from the paper. Even if your child is left-handed,
this will not be a problem.

6

★ The Letters **a, c, e, o,** and **s**

FACTS Groups of letters that have similar shapes, curves, or lines
are sometimes called letter families.

Write the letters with round shapes. Trace each letter.
Then write more letters on each line until you fill the line.
Start at the dots and follow the arrows.

Write round letters to finish the picture.

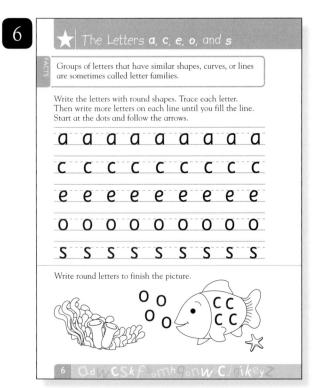

Writing letters again and again will build
familiarity with shape and formation.
The letters should all be the same height
and "sit" on the lines.

The Letters **d, g,** and **q** ★

The letters **d, g,** and **q** begin with a round shape. Trace the
letter **d** by starting at the dots and following the arrows.
Write more letters until you fill the line.

Write the letters **g** and **q**. Trace them by starting at the dots
and following the arrows. Write more letters on each line.
Remember: The round part of each letter sits on the line.
The bottom part goes down under the line.

The letter **g** looks like a hook. Trace the letter **g**. Then write
the letter **g** three more times to finish the picture. Start each
letter from the end of the fishing line.

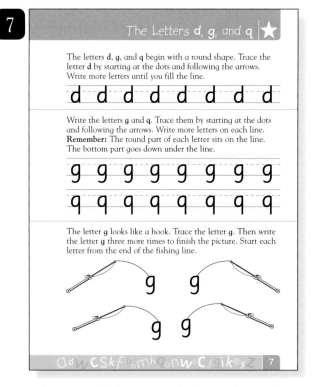

When your child is tracing the letters **d, g,** and
q on this page, introduce the terms "ascender"
and "descender." Ascenders are parts of the letters
that go above the body of the letter. Descenders
are parts of the letters that go below the body of
the letter.

★ The Letters **f**, **i**, **j**, **l**, and **t**

Write the letters **f**, **l**, and **t**. Trace them and then write more letters to fill the lines. Start at the dots and follow the arrows for direction. **Remember:** Write the bar or the line that goes across the letters **f** and **t**, last.

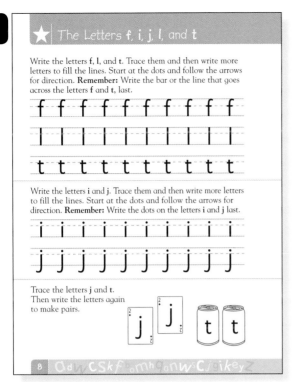

Write the letters **i** and **j**. Trace them and then write more letters to fill the lines. Start at the dots and follow the arrows for direction. **Remember:** Write the dots on the letters **i** and **j** last.

Trace the letters **j** and **t**. Then write the letters again to make pairs.

Ensure that your child writes the main strokes of the letters **f**, **i**, **j**, and **t** first, adding dots and bars last. Also, remember that the letter **f** can be written in different ways, depending on the handwriting style taught in school.

9

The Letters **m**, **n**, and **r** ★

Write the letters **m**, **n**, and **r**. Trace them and then write more letters to fill the lines. Start at the dots and follow the arrows for direction. **Remember:** Your letters should all be the same height.

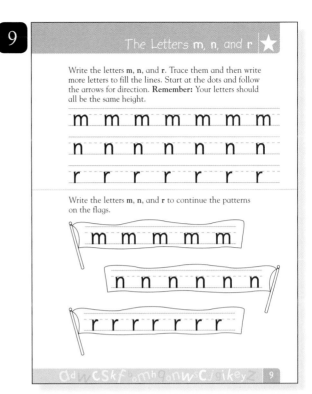

Write the letters **m**, **n**, and **r** to continue the patterns on the flags.

Help your child develop consistency in letter formation. Ensure that the letters are uniform in size, height, and shape.

10

★ The Letters **b**, **h**, **k**, and **p**

Write the letters **b** and **h**. Trace them and then write more letters to fill the lines. Start at the dots and follow the arrows for direction. **Remember:** Your letters should all be the same height.

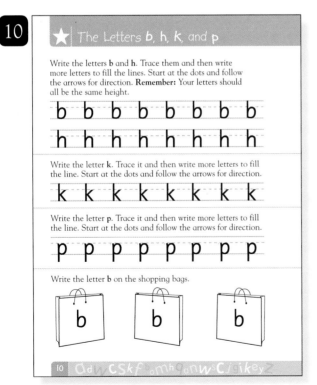

Write the letter **k**. Trace it and then write more letters to fill the line. Start at the dots and follow the arrows for direction.

Write the letter **p**. Trace it and then write more letters to fill the line. Start at the dots and follow the arrows for direction.

Write the letter **b** on the shopping bags.

Explain the words "ascender" and "descender" to your child again so that these become familiar terms.

11

The Letters **u**, **v**, **w**, **x**, **y**, and **z** ★

Write the straight-line letters **v**, **w**, **x**, and **z**. Trace them and then write more letters to fill the lines. Start at the dots and follow the arrows for direction.

Write the letters **u** and **y**. Trace them and then write more letters to fill the lines. Start at the dots and follow the arrows for direction.

Copy the letters again.

Talk about the characteristics of letters with your child, comparing the spiked, straight-line letters **v**, **w**, **x**, and **z** with the more rounded **u** and **y**.

Trace each letter of the alphabet and then write it two more times. **Remember:** The alphabet is all the letters we use to make words.

Always praise your child's handwriting efforts and remember that some children are naturally neater than others. In handwriting, practice really does improve skill.

Trace the letters of the alphabet in order. Write as neatly as you can. **Remember:** Some lowercase letters go up to the top line (l); some go halfway up (a); some have parts that are round (c, o); and some have parts that are straight and parts that are round (b and d).

If your child is unsure of the sequence of strokes in letter formation, turn to the previous pages for guidance. Provide lined paper for further practice.

Use the correct letter from the box to begin each word below. Then write the whole word.

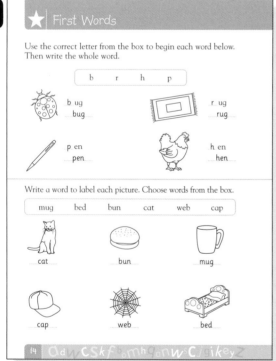

Reading, writing, and spelling are very closely linked. Good handwriting, good reading, and good spelling develop naturally together. Handwriting practice supports all English language arts skills.

Write these words that have the letter **a** in the middle. They all make the short "a" sound, as heard in "bat." Write each word three times.

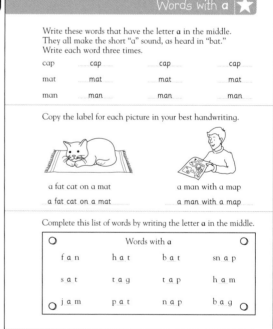

Your child should practice writing CVC (consonant-vowel-consonant) words with the short "a" sound, as in "pan," by either copying a list of words or writing them independently. Offer help if needed.

★ Words with *e*

Complete each row by writing a word with the letter **e** in the middle. Then copy all the words in your best handwriting on the lines below. **Remember:** The words in each row should rhyme. The endings of these words should sound the same.

yet	set	......e......
yet	set	*Answers may vary*
led	fed	
led	fed	

Copy the label for each picture in your best handwriting.

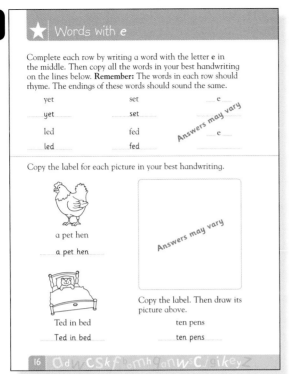

a pet hen

a pet hen

Answers may vary

Copy the label. Then draw its picture above.

Ted in bed

Ted in bed

ten pens

ten pens

Help your child recognize patterns in the sets of rhyming CVC words with the short "e" vowel sound. The goal is for your child to be able to write rhyming words independently. The drawing exercise will help develop pencil control.

Words with *i* ★

Write these words that have the letter **i** in the middle. They all make the short "i" sound, as heard in "pin."

fin	fin	fin	fin
sit	sit	sit	sit
bib	bib	bib	bib

Complete this list of words by writing the letter **i** in the middle.

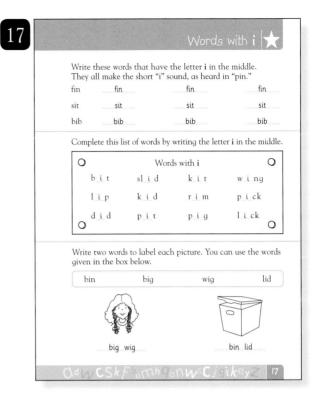

	Words with **i**		
b i t	s l i d	k i t	w i ng
l i p	k i d	r i m	p i ck
d i d	p i t	p i g	l i ck

Write two words to label each picture. You can use the words given in the box below.

| bin | big | wig | lid |

big wig

bin lid

This page focuses on words with the short "i" sound, as in "pin." Knowing the spellings of words builds a child's confidence and independence when writing.

★ Words with *o*

Complete the row by writing a word with the letter **o** in the middle. Then write all the words in your best handwriting on the lines. **Remember:** The words in the row should rhyme. Their endings should sound the same. **Answers may vary**

| dot | pot | ......o...... |
| dot | pot | |

Write a label for each picture. Try to write more than one word for each label. Use words from the box and other words of your own. **Answers may vary**

| toy | log | rock | boy | dots | dog | frog | box |

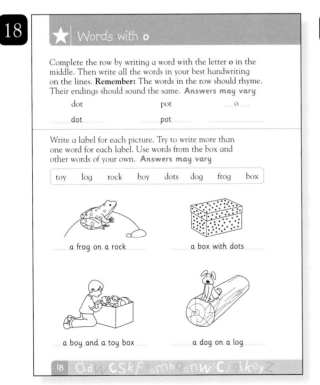

a frog on a rock

a box with dots

a boy and a toy box

a dog on a log

Help your child write words that follow the same spelling pattern, with the letter **o** in the middle. For example: "fog," "log," and "dog." Offer help writing phrases rather than single words when labeling pictures.

Words with *u* ★

Write these words that have the letter **u** in the middle. They all make the short "u" sound, as heard in "bun."

fun	fun	fun	fun
tub	tub	tub	tub
bud	bud	bud	bud
jug	jug	jug	jug

Write a label for each picture. Try to write more than one word for each label. Use the **u** words from the box and other words of your own. **Answers may vary**

| pup | bug | rug | cup |

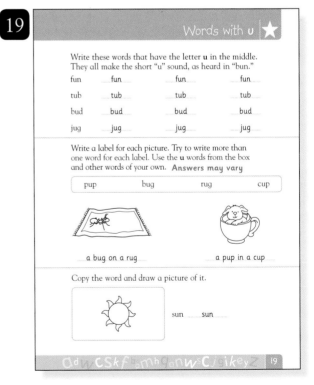

a bug on a rug

a pup in a cup

Copy the word and draw a picture of it.

sun ......sun......

The focus of this page is the short vowel sound—"u" as in "sum"—in CVC words. Writing familiar words again and again will build the confidence your child needs to write phrases independently.

★ Letter Blends

FACTS

Some words have two or more letters whose sounds blend together. You can hear the sound of each letter. Letter blends include **bl** in the word "blue" and **fl** in the word "flower."

Copy these letter blends that start words.

bl	fr	gr	cr	sl	sc	st	sm	sn	sp
bl	fr	gr	cr	sl	sc	st	sm	sn	sp

Copy these letter blends that end words.

ft	nt	xt	lf	ct	lt	pt	nd	lp	st
ft	nt	xt	lf	ct	lt	pt	nd	lp	st

Copy these words that have letter blends.

spot	spot	flag	flag	band	band
frog	frog	fact	fact	next	next
star	star	brick	brick	snake	snake

Write these words that have letter blends. Then circle the letter blends at the beginning or end of each word.

drum
d(r)um

nest
ne(st)

Explain to your child that "consonant" is the term for all the letters of the alphabet, except the vowels **a**, **e**, **i**, **o**, **u**, and sometimes **y**. Point out examples of any two letter sounds blending to make a new one, such as "g" + "r" = "gr."

Final Consonants ★

FACTS

Some words end in two consonants. Those final consonants may be the same letter twice, as in "bell," or be different, as in "jump."

Copy these words that end with two letters that are the same.

off	off	puff	puff	bell	bell
pull	pull	dress	dress	kiss	kiss

Copy these words that end with **ck**, **mp**, and **ng**.

sock	sock	wing	wing	duck	duck
jump	jump	sing	sing	ring	ring

Write labels for the pictures. Use the words from above.

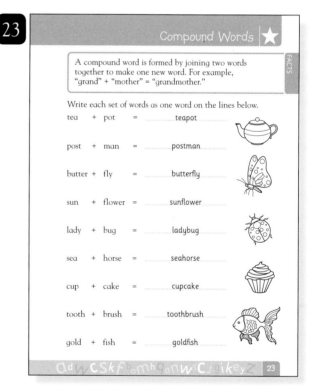

bell   dress   duck

sock   ring   jump

Make sure that your child practices writing familiar and useful words given on this page. It will develop and improve handwriting. It will also support your child's reading and spelling skills.

★ Family Words

Write each word three times on the lines below.
Remember: Always write the word "I" as an uppercase (big) letter. For example, "I like to write words."

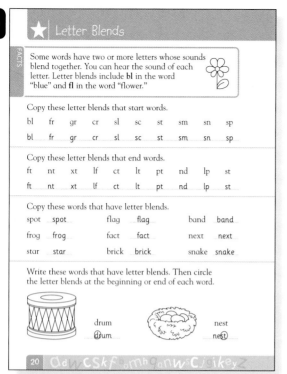

I	I	I	I
me	me	me	me
he	he	he	he
we	we	we	we
she	she	she	she

Write labels for this family. Choose words from the box.

mom	dad	baby	girl

dad   girl   mom   baby

Write your first name.   **Answers may vary**
Write your last name.   **Answers may vary**

Writing common words again and again gives your child the opportunity to become familiar with their "feel" and formation. The aim of these exercises is to help your child improve handwriting conformity.

Compound Words ★

FACTS

A compound word is formed by joining two words together to make one new word. For example, "grand" + "mother" = "grandmother."

Write each set of words as one word on the lines below.

tea	+	pot	=	teapot
post	+	man	=	postman
butter	+	fly	=	butterfly
sun	+	flower	=	sunflower
lady	+	bug	=	ladybug
sea	+	horse	=	seahorse
cup	+	cake	=	cupcake
tooth	+	brush	=	toothbrush
gold	+	fish	=	goldfish

Explain the term "compound words" to your child. Activities like this introduce a play element into handwriting practice. Help your child find words that can be put together and write them as compound words. Look for pictures that provide clues for some words.

★ Classroom Words

Write each classroom word three times. Try to keep your handwriting the same size as the words you are copying.

book	book	book	book
desk	desk	desk	desk
chair	chair	chair	chair
pencil	pencil	pencil	pencil
clock	clock	clock	clock
paints	paints	paints	paints
bin	bin	bin	bin
teacher	teacher	teacher	teacher
paper	paper	paper	paper
bag	bag	bag	bag

Write labels for the pictures.

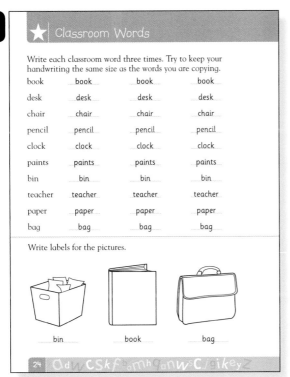

bin   book   bag

Not all children will be familiar with the names of classroom items. Writing them more than once will help your child spell them and use them with confidence later. It will also improve handwriting.

Color Words ★

Write the color words below three times.

red	red	red	red
green	green	green	green
yellow	yellow	yellow	yellow
blue	blue	blue	blue
black	black	black	black
white	white	white	white
orange	orange	orange	orange
pink	pink	pink	pink
brown	brown	brown	brown
gray	gray	gray	gray

The word "blue" begins with a blend. Write four other color words that begin with a blend.

black   green

brown   gray

Complete the following sentence.
My favorite color is   because

Answers may vary

Writing commonly used words, such as color words, more than once will help your child build and consolidate handwriting skills. This exercise will also improve reading and spelling skills.

★ Numbers

FACTS: Numerals are the symbols we use for numbers.

Write the numerals from 0 to 20 on the lines below.
Note: Sometimes 4 is also written as 4.

| 0 | 1 | 2 | 3 | 4 | 5 | 6 | 7 | 8 | 9 | 10 |
| 0 | 1 | 2 | 3 | 4 | 5 | 6 | 7 | 8 | 9 | 10 |

| 11 | 12 | 13 | 14 | 15 | 16 | 17 | 18 | 19 | 20 |
| 11 | 12 | 13 | 14 | 15 | 16 | 17 | 18 | 19 | 20 |

Write the number words from zero to twenty.

zero	zero		
one	one	eleven	eleven
two	two	twelve	twelve
three	three	thirteen	thirteen
four	four	fourteen	fourteen
five	five	fifteen	fifteen
six	six	sixteen	sixteen
seven	seven	seventeen	seventeen
eight	eight	eighteen	eighteen
nine	nine	nineteen	nineteen
ten	ten	twenty	twenty

When your child comes to this page, you may need to explain the terms "numerals" and "number words." Provide extra sheets of lined paper for further practice. If your child is tired or bored, revisit the activities at another time.

Numbers ★

Write a number word label for each numeral shown on the balloons. One has been done for you.

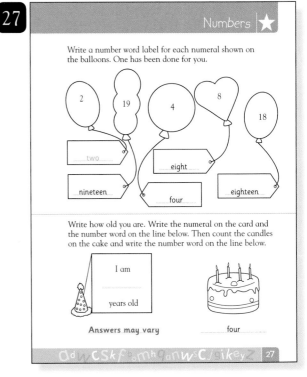

two   eight   nineteen   four   eighteen

Write how old you are. Write the numeral on the card and the number word on the line below. Then count the candles on the cake and write the number word on the line below.

I am

years old

Answers may vary   four

Talk about the practical uses of handwriting with your child, for example, in recording personal details, such as names and addresses on forms, and in writing cards and letters.

★ The "ai," "ee," and "ie" Sounds

FACTS

Different spelling patterns can make the same sound. For example, the "ai" sound, as heard in "main," can also be spelled "ay," as in "say," and "a_e," as in "late."

Copy these words that have the "ai" sound, as heard in "train."

tail   tail   rain   rain

day   day   plate   plate

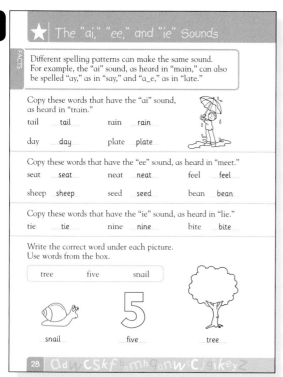

Copy these words that have the "ee" sound, as heard in "meet."

seat   seat   neat   neat   feel   feel

sheep   sheep   seed   seed   bean   bean

Copy these words that have the "ie" sound, as heard in "lie."

tie   tie   nine   nine   bite   bite

Write the correct word under each picture.
Use words from the box.

tree	five	snail

snail   five   tree

Through exposure and repetition, your child will learn to identify, write, and differentiate between words that make the same sound but are spelled differently. Encourage clear, neat writing.

The "oa" and "oo" Sounds ★

Copy these words that have the "oa" sound, as heard in "coat."

home   home   moat   moat   goat   goat

low   low   road   road   note   note

soap   soap   snow   snow   show   show

Copy these words that have the "oo" sound, as heard in "soon."

moon   moon   spoon   spoon   bloom   bloom

blue   blue   true   true   glue   glue

flew   flew   rule   rule   pool   pool

Copy these sentences in your best handwriting.
Remember: A sentence begins with an uppercase letter and ends with a period.

The dish ran away with the spoon.

The dish ran away with the spoon.

The goat plays in the snow.

The goat plays in the snow.

Encourage your child to write full sentences, using the uppercase letters and end punctuation. This will ensure uniform handwriting. Remember to praise good letter formation and neat work.

★ The "ar" Sound

Sometimes the letters **ar** make the sound heard in the word "car." Write the words with the "ar" sound below three times.

farm   farm   farm   farm

art   art   art   art

cart   cart   cart   cart

chart   chart   chart   chart

barn   barn   barn   barn

bark   bark   bark   bark

shark   shark   shark   shark

party   party   party   party

sharp   sharp   sharp   sharp

Write the word with the "ar" sound that names each picture.

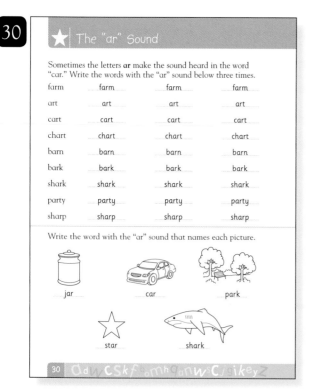

jar   car   park

star   shark

After writing lots of "ar" words again and again, your child should be able to write labels independently. Offer help with spelling or use a wordbook and dictionary together.

The "oo," "oy," and "ow" Sounds ★

Copy these words with the short "oo" sound, as heard in "good."

hood   hood   wood   wood   could   could

push   push   pull   pull   would   would

wool   wool   full   full   should   should

Copy these words with the "oy" sound, as heard in "toy."

boy   boy   boil   boil   soil   soil

joy   joy   foil   foil   coil   coil

coin   coin   spoil   spoil   enjoy   enjoy

Copy these words with the "ow" sound, as heard in "now."

out   out   town   town   towel   towel

cow   cow   loud   loud   found   found

owl   owl   now   now   shout   shout

Write the words for the two pictures.

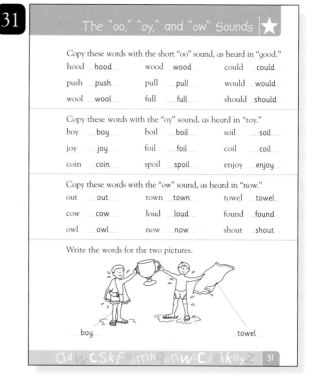

boy   towel

Talk to your child and point out how different sets of letters can make the same sound, such as the "oo," "oy," and "ow" sounds. Activities such as these will build your child's vocabulary and help improve spelling skills.

★ The Uppercase Alphabet

FACTS

Uppercase letters are big letters. Some words, such as "I," the names of people (John), and the names of places (Arizona), begin with uppercase letters. Uppercase letters are also called capital letters.

Write the alphabet in uppercase letters on the lines.
Start at the dots and follow the arrows for direction.
Remember: The alphabet starts with **A** and ends with **Z**.

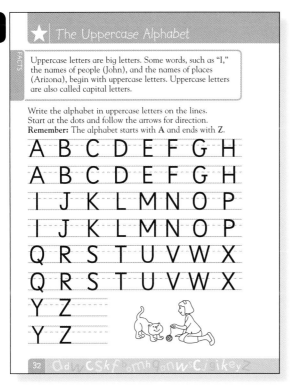

Talk about the appropriate use of uppercase letters with your child. Make a game of spotting them in different places, for instance, in newspapers or on street signs.

Proper Nouns ★

FACTS

Proper nouns are words that name people and places. They always begin with an uppercase letter.

Write these names in your best handwriting.

Eric	Eric	Will	Will
Tom	Tom	Mel	Mel
Sam	Sam	Lucy	Lucy
Katy	Katy	Ben	Ben
Tim	Tim	Jemma	Jemma

Write your name. **Answers may vary**
Make a list of your friends' names.

My Friends

Answers may vary

The focus of this page is using uppercase and lowercase letters in proper nouns. Point out a variety of appropriate uses of uppercase letters. For example, in names of places, addresses, and street signs.

★ More Uppercase Letters

A lowercase letter is written on each flower. Write the uppercase form of the letter on the leaves of each flower, as shown for the letter **a**.

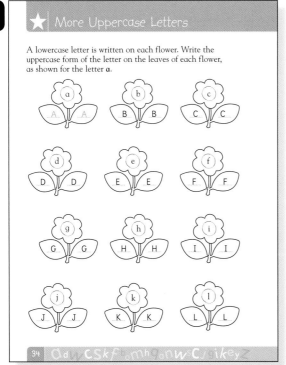

On pages 34 and 35 your child should write sets of uppercase letters on the dotted lines to match the lowercase letters printed on the flowers.

More Uppercase Letters ★

If your child is in doubt, revisit page 32 for the correct formation and stroke sequence of the letters.

★ Sentences

FACTS

A sentence is a group of words that forms a complete thought. Every sentence starts with an uppercase letter and ends with a period (.), a question mark (?), or an exclamation point (!).

Write these sentences in your best handwriting.

I like plums.   I like plums.

I can jump.   I can jump.

I like to write.   I like to write.

Write these words as sentences. **Remember:** You may want to put a finger-width space between each word to make your writing easier to read.

i just won the trophy

I just won the trophy!

how old is dan

How old is Dan?

i like my new bike

I like my new bike.

the cat is black

The cat is black.

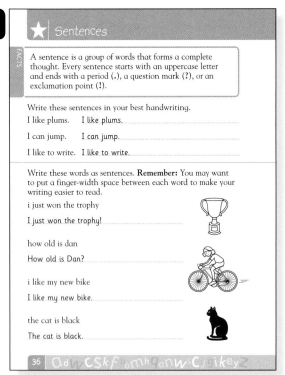

Help your child recognize, understand, and use terms, such as "sentence," "uppercase letter," and "period." Encourage neat, careful handwriting.

The Days of the Week ★

FACTS

The names of the days of the week are proper nouns. Each starts with an uppercase letter.

Copy the names of the days of the week in your neatest handwriting. Write each name twice.

Sunday	Sunday	Sunday
Monday	Monday	Monday
Tuesday	Tuesday	Tuesday
Wednesday	Wednesday	Wednesday
Thursday	Thursday	Thursday
Friday	Friday	Friday
Saturday	Saturday	Saturday

Write the name of the day that comes after Friday.   Saturday

Which days begin with **T**?   Tuesday, Thursday

On which days do you go to school? Monday, Tuesday, Wednesday, Thursday, and Friday

What is the day today? Write what you have done so far today.

Answers may vary

Point out the use of uppercase letters. Your child will need to use them frequently in schoolwork when writing the days of the week. Explain that all the words break into smaller parts, or syllables. For example, Friday = Fri + day.

★ The Months of the Year

Copy the names of the months of the year twice.
Remember: Months are proper nouns. They start with an uppercase letter.

January	January	January
February	February	February
March	March	March
April	April	April
May	May	May
June	June	June
July	July	July
August	August	August
September	September	September
October	October	October
November	November	November
December	December	December

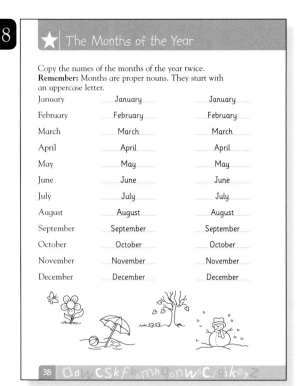

Explain the use of uppercase letters in proper nouns. Ask your child to write the useful—but long—words given on this page by looking for and recognizing common letter patterns in spellings. Point out similar word endings, such as "-ember" and "-ary."

Titles ★

The title of a book, story, or rhyme is its name. Write these titles in your best handwriting. **Remember:** Begin main words in titles with uppercase letters.

James and the Giant Peach

James and the Giant Peach

Old Macdonald Had a Farm

Old Macdonald Had a Farm

Write a title for each cover from the list below.

Old King Cole   In a Dark, Dark Wood

Goldilocks and
the Three Bears

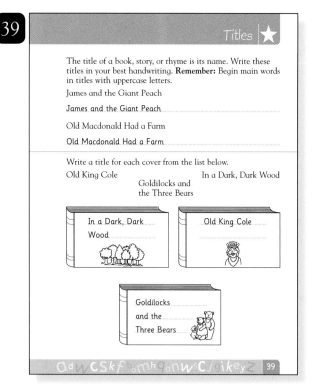

In a Dark, Dark Wood

Old King Cole

Goldilocks and the Three Bears

Look at different examples of printed lettering and handwriting styles with your child—including yours! Explore forms and styles of print in magazines, comic books, and books.

★ A Poem

Draw a picture and copy the poem in your best handwriting. Begin by writing the title. **Remember:** Write in uppercase and lowercase letters. Use commas and periods.

Little Wind
Little wind, blow on the hilltop,
Little wind, blow on the plain,
Little wind, blow up the sunshine,
Little wind, blow off the rain.
Anonymous

Answers may vary

Little Wind
Little wind, blow on the hilltop,
Little wind, blow on the plain,
Little wind, blow up the sunshine,
Little wind, blow off the rain.
Anonymous

Always praise your child's efforts in handwriting and stress the positive details. Ask your child to write and illustrate a second version of the poem, and pin it up on the wall or frame it.

Punctuation ★

FACTS
A comma is a punctuation mark that is used to show a break in the sentence or a slight pause. Commas are also used to separate words in a list. For example, "I like apples, bananas, and cherries."

The commas in this rhyme show you when to pause. Copy the rhyme in your best handwriting.

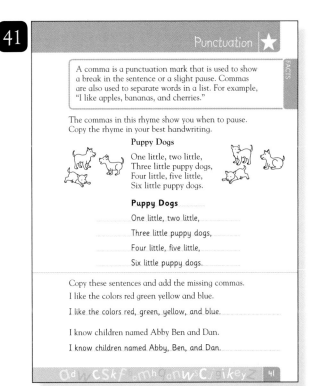

Puppy Dogs
One little, two little,
Three little puppy dogs,
Four little, five little,
Six little puppy dogs.

Puppy Dogs
One little, two little,
Three little puppy dogs,
Four little, five little,
Six little puppy dogs.

Copy these sentences and add the missing commas.
I like the colors red green yellow and blue.
I like the colors red, green, yellow, and blue.

I know children named Abby Ben and Dan.
I know children named Abby, Ben, and Dan.

Encourage your child to get into the habit of rereading written work, checking it for uniformity in handwriting and regular spacing between words. Point out the importance of using correct punctuation.

★ More Punctuation

FACTS
A question mark (?) is used in a sentence that asks a question. An exclamation point (!) shows anger, pain, danger, or excitement.

Rewrite each sentence with a question mark or an exclamation point at the end.

Do you like apples
Do you like apples?

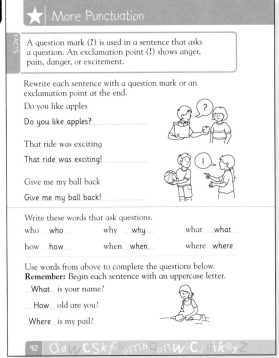

That ride was exciting
That ride was exciting!

Give me my ball back
Give me my ball back!

Write these words that ask questions.
who who   why why   what what
how how   when when   where where

Use words from above to complete the questions below.
Remember: Begin each sentence with an uppercase letter.
What is your name?
How old are you?
Where is my pail?

Your child should practice writing words that ask questions. On this page, have your child complete the sentences by writing the missing words. Point out question words in other books, too. Provide practice sentences that use question marks and exclamation points.

Fiction and Nonfiction ★

FACTS
Books that are made up are called fiction. The stories are not real. Books that are true are called nonfiction. They give information and facts.

Copy these book titles using uppercase and lowercase letters.
Remember: The title is the name of the book.

Fiction	Nonfiction
The Ugly Duckling	My Book of Space
The Ugly Duckling	My Book of Space
The Snowman	How to Draw
The Snowman	How to Draw
Old Bear	Learn about Tigers
Old Bear	Learn about Tigers
The Worst Witch	Fun with Numbers
The Worst Witch	Fun with Numbers

Find the title on the list above and write it on each book cover.

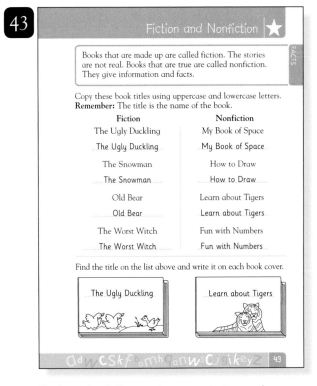

The Ugly Duckling

Learn about Tigers

Explain the difference between fiction and nonfiction writing to your child. Read books together and point out how uppercase and lowercase letters are used for titles, authors' names, chapter names, and so on.

★ Story Writing

Write a short story in your best handwriting. Look at the pictures and write a sentence about each one. Use the words given in the box. **Remember:** A sentence begins with an uppercase letter and ends with a period, question mark, or exclamation point. **Answers may vary**

| boy | girl | build | snowman | night | day |

Title: _____

Taking clues from the pictures, your child should talk about events in the story and then plan what to write. These are important steps in independent writing. Offer your help with spelling. Remind your child to give a title to the story.

Information Books ★

FACTS

A dictionary is a book that tells you what words mean.

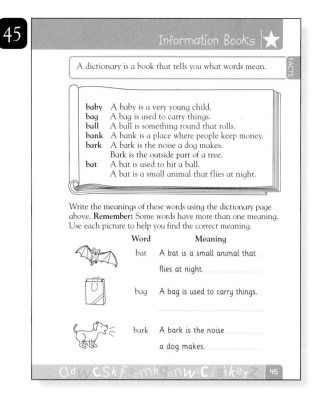

Write the meanings of these words using the dictionary page above. **Remember:** Some words have more than one meaning. Use each picture to help you find the correct meaning.

	Word	Meaning
	bat	A bat is a small animal that flies at night.
	bag	A bag is used to carry things.
	bark	A bark is the noise a dog makes.

Dictionaries and wordbooks are really useful additions to the family bookshelf. Encourage neat and accurate writing and make sure that the word meanings are written out in complete sentences.

★ Topic Work

Write each word in the correct topic box. Use your neatest handwriting.

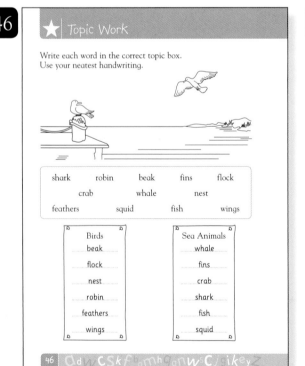

shark	robin	beak	fins	flock
crab	whale	nest		
feathers	squid	fish	wings	

Birds
beak
flock
nest
robin
feathers
wings

Sea Animals
whale
fins
crab
shark
fish
squid

Topic work will feature regularly in your child's schoolwork. It involves categorizing words to make lists. Help your child by reading and spelling any unfamiliar words. Encourage your child to create word lists.

Personal Information ★

Write about yourself in your best handwriting and draw a picture. **Remember:** Proper nouns begin with uppercase letters.

Name: _____
Street: _____
Town or city: _____
State: _____
Zip code: _____
Age: _____
Date of birth: _____
School: _____
Grade: _____
Favorite subject: _____
Teacher's name: _____

Answers may vary

This page records your child's successful completion of the handwriting activities in this book. Look back at all the activities together. Note your child's progress and offer praise.